BRITAIN'S RAILWAY

—— THE ONLY TRANSPORT FOR THE FUTURE ——

by
Colin Garratt

"The disintegration of British Rail is an act of political imbecility; a squalid opting out of responsibility to the nation and its industrial infrastructure"

First published 1993 by Sunburst Books, Deacon House, 65 Old Church Street, London, SW3 5BS.

© Sunburst Books 1993

© Illustrations/photographs Milepost 92½ 1993

© Design Sunburst Books 1993

ISBN 1 85778 020 5

Printed and bound in Great Britain

CONTENTS

A happy scene when West Yorkshire PTE enabled the reopening of the Wakefield- Pontefract line to passengers in 1992

INTRODUCTION

Britain's Railway is a celebration of British Rail's operation and achievements to date. It has transformed itself from a bureaucratic monolith into a progressive hi-tech business divided into six manageable operating sectors independently accountable for performance and cost-effectiveness. The sectors InterCity, Regional Railways, Network SouthEast, Post and Parcels, Railfreight Distribution, Trainload Freight, own their assets - track, property, personnel and trains.

Sectorisation is ensuring a clear accountability, totally decentralised management structure and a vigorous marketing strategy which by the day is evolving into an ever more successful customer-orientated service with an ever increasing sense of pride, identity and responsibility.

"Cuts will savage the national timetable prior to fragmentation of the network in 1994"

The creation of these sectors in 1992 under Organising for Quality (OFQ) has been the most dramatic reconstruction of our railway since it moved into state ownership forty-five years ago.
The sense of identity and commitment within these six sectors has become so intense that British Rail as such barely exists, yet the system remains vitally unified under the British Railways Board which oversees the crucial issue of safety, investment, strategy, and planning of new lines, along with the diverse range of technical skills and research from Central Services.

Without enlightened railway development our target for greenhouse gas emissions cannot be met. Cities will become increasingly polluted and congested. Britain's annual road accident toll of 4,500 dead and hundreds of thousands seriously injured will increase

An average family car costs 60p a mile to run (AA figures). Rail travel averages 15p a mile

The East Coast MainLine is largely operated by luxurious InterCity 225 trains capable of running from London- Edinburgh in under 4 hours

Manchester's Metrolink joins with Regional railways and InterCity underscoring the limitless potential for railway development by the forecast rise in motor traffic of 142% in less than two decades.

Railways are up to four times more energy-efficient than roads. They take one third of land space to convey the same number of people and they provide a safe disciplined form of transport for everyone. With only 60 per cent of the population owning cars they are essential.

The unfair basis on which the true cost of rail and road operations are assessed has done much to distort transport policies over recent years. Society pays dearly for its roads in Policing, accidents, construction, maintenance - all coming from public funds, whereas a rail ticket or freight tariff bears a direct relationship to its total cost.

"The mischief of privatisation has done more to damage and demoralise our railway than Hitler's Luftwaffe ever did"

The Victorians planned our residential, commercial and industrial developments around the railway network. So should we, but the post-war years have seen an abandonment of this principle. New towns have sprung up away from rail links and out-of-town industrial estates and hypermarkets have exacerbated use of the car and lorry, enabling politicians to claim tritely that the railway cannot handle the nation's transport needs.

The need has never been greater for a properly integrated railway network operating under a coherent national transport policy. So what do rail managers do? Accept the disintegration of the network and pick up the pieces afterwards, or rebel at the erosion of the railway?

It is irresponsible to contend that British Rail has a monopoly - it competes on an unequal basis against cars, coaches, planes and heavy trucking.

There exists within British Rail a professional commitment and devotion to the industry along with a plethora of hi-tech skills and knowledge which, could so easily - even at this eleventh hour - make our

Sheffield's Meadowhall is a perfect- and all too rare- example of a major shopping complex properly integrated with public transport

ABB are leaders in urban transit. Part of
a contract for 700 vehicles for London
Underground's Central Line.

The Networker Revolution heralded a new generation of cost-effective trains

ABB Transportation Limited build many of Britain's prestigious trains.

"Using computer-aided design, fresh concepts in railway engineering are pioneered for improved efficiency, passenger safety and comfort"

There are three fields of operation: the construction of new vehicles, the manufacture of bogies and the repair and rehabilitation of rolling stock and equipment. The Company operates from sites in York, Crewe and Derby, towns with one and a half centuries of railway tradition. Since 1970 the company has won orders for over 2,700 main-line coaches, 4,500 diesel and electrical multiple-units, 500 locomotives and 700 metro cars.

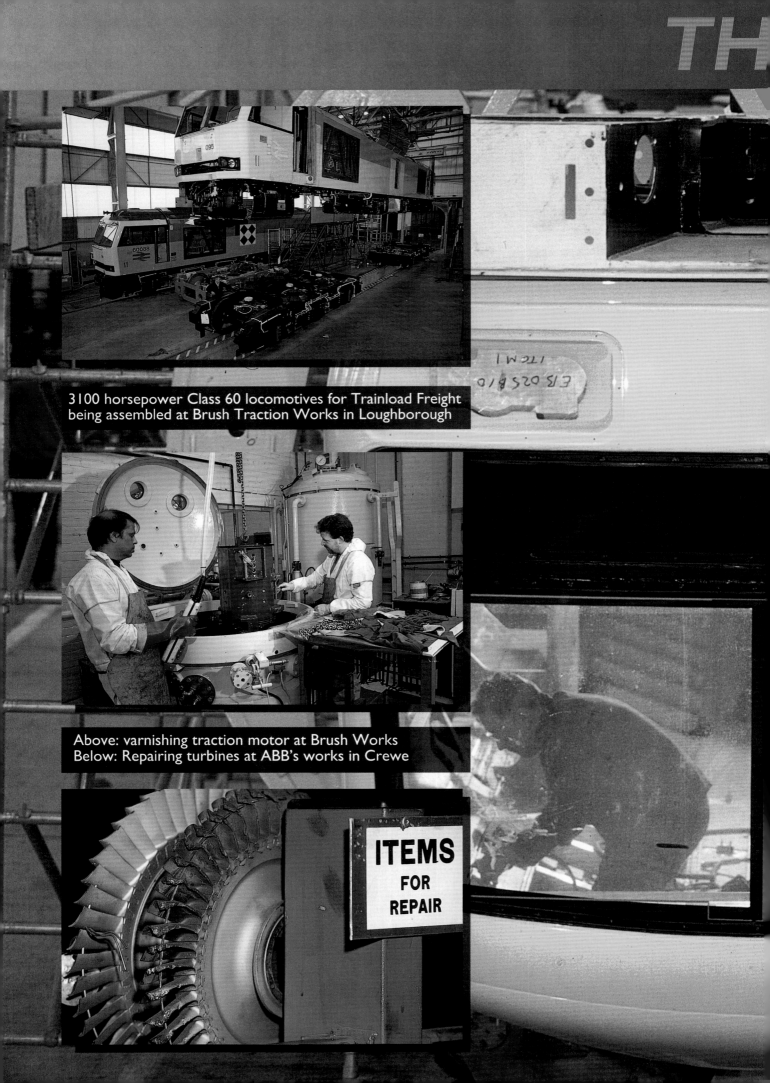

3100 horsepower Class 60 locomotives for Trainload Freight
being assembled at Brush Traction Works in Loughborough

Above: varnishing traction motor at Brush Works
Below: Repairing turbines at ABB's works in Crewe

ITEMS
FOR
REPAIR

York is Britain's leading builder of multiple-unit trains: Thameslink's dual-voltage 319s, the Wessex Electrics and the 321 family.

These are steel-bodied vehicles but the Networker revolution which began in 1990 introduced aluminium for strength, lightness and speed of construction.

"Threatened privatisation means that no new trains are on order. Accordingly, Britain's railway building industry could be annihilated by 1995"

Business at the legendary Crewe works includes the overhaul of locomotives, wagons and power units. These come from many sources including British Rail, Industrial Operators and the Ministry of Defence.

Derby is the home of ABB Transportation Limited's bogie division which has brought the company great distinction.

At Derby Carriage Works over 400 Class 158s were built as the flagship of Regional Railways.

The present situation facing ABB is bleak - its works at Crewe, Derby and York are not fully occupied as privatisation proposals, combined with the Government's economic policy, have prevented British Rail and London Underground Limited placing orders for new trains. Without these orders, York and Derby will run out of new construction work by the end of 1994.

"The loss of our railway manufacturing industry would be many nails in the coffin of Britain's economic and industrial future"

The lead time for design and project managing of any new build is far longer than the existing leeway. Once the skilled manpower essential to so specialised an industry has gone, Britain will not only have to import railway equipment, but with the home industry decimated our capacity to export will be almost non-existent.

Each train has a dedicated team; the driver, a senior conductor to provide customer assistance, along with a chief steward and his crew

Its easy to buy a ticket; by cash, cheque or credit card from your local travel agent, station or even by telephone. Seats can be reserved too

INTERCITY

InterCity stations are welcoming and easy to use

By any standards InterCity is a magnificent service; a prestigious organisation and one of Britain's top 150 companies. Civilised travel, city centre to city centre. A 3,500 mile network linking Britain's principal high speed services; it is the only long-distance passenger railway in the world to operate at a profit; it runs the fastest diesel trains in the world and competes successfully against other forms of transport by providing

"InterCity is the only long-distance passenger network in the world to run at a profit"

towns and cities from Aberdeen and Inverness in the North to Poole and Penzance in the South.

The key to its success is frequent direct, stress-free travel across the nation. Seats can be reserved and for leisure travellers Apex, Super Apex Savers and Super Savers give huge reductions on standard fares, whilst

railcards for children, students, seniors citizens, families and the disabled give further discounts. Seventy per cent. travel on leisure, 30 per cent. on business.

All trains have catering ranging from a trolley or buffet to a full meal service with a choice of market researched menus. Buffets stock ten brands of beer and cider, thirteen brands of spirits and sixty varieties of sandwiches - many delicacies in their own right under the signature of Clement Freud. The wine range, like sandwiches and other products, is also chosen by a panel of experts.

InterCity is becoming more customer-orientated by the day with excellent standards of cleanliness and punctuality, highly trained senior conductors on all trains with facilities like on board telephones and Hertz Car Rental being available throughout the network.

Aware of how important its services are to business travellers, InterCity has many exciting plans to make them even more attractive including stewardesses to greet passengers and shuttle services

"InterCity has a brand name synonymous with quality and copied all over the world"

InterCity enables business people to make proper use of their time, either to work, conduct meetings or relax and reflect in comfort as the panorama unfolds. Few companies can afford to have their executives wasting time behind the wheel of a car.

InterCity stations are welcoming and easy to use - car parking, superb travel centres, information areas, self help luggage trolleys, clear signs and provision for the disabled including induction loops for the hard of hearing.

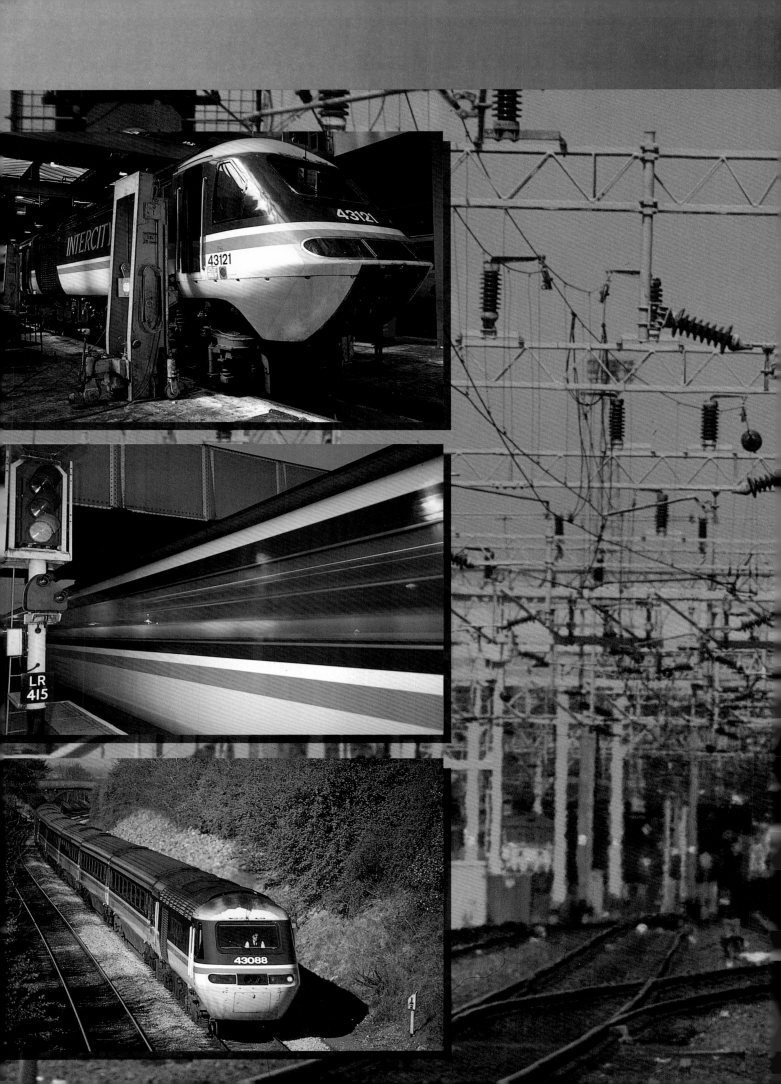

INTERCITY

InterCity coaches are carpeted, air conditioned and double glazed. Pullman lounges are located at five key stations offering light refreshments and business services such as telephone and fax.

It is widely acknowledged within the industry that InterCity's Director, Chris Green, is one of the greatest railwaymen of all time - and Britain can

"InterCity 125 is the fastest diesel train in the world"

boast many over almost two centuries of railway innovation.

New technology and investment would easily ensure that InterCity stays at the forefront of world railways.

The century-old Forth Bridge; 54,000 tonnes of steel containing 7 million rivets and standing higher than St. Paul's Cathedral

New trains are spacious and air-conditioned with panoramic low-silled anti-glare windows

There's an at-seat trolley catering service with an excellent selection of snacks and drinks

GIONAL RAILWAYS

REGIONAL RAILWAYS

Regional Railways has a key role in the development of public transport. Its aims are threefold - to provide: urban rail services in cities outside London and the South East, Interurban services linking towns and cities, and to maintain connections with rural communities.

third from a governmental public services obligation grant, and the remainder from local government controlled Passenger Transport Executives - known as PTE's - who pay Regional Railways to operate their services. Financial support is also given by local authorities for specific

"Regional Railways is the fastest growing passenger rail business in the country"

Regional Railways has five business units: ScotRail, North West, North East, Central, and South Wales and West. Each runs from its own base with the main office in Birmingham.

projects such as the re-opening of the Ivanhoe Line between Leicester and Burton-Upon-Trent and the Robin Hood Line in Nottinghamshire.

"Regional Railways is coordinated, it has a tangible marketing strategy and is a major force in Britain's Railway"

Regional Railways operates 53 per cent of British Rail's route mileage and has almost 1500 stations. A third of its £700m turnover comes from fares; a

When the business sector was formed in 1982, it inherited old rolling-stock and run-down lines. Today the average age of diesel trains is only

Most Rural Service trains have power-operated doors, a p.a. system and toilets for the disabled

seven years. The new livery is modern and eye-catching and has a high public profile with trains instantly recognisable.

THE URBAN SERVICE

The Urban Service covers the main population areas including PTE trains. The aim is to beat congestion and keep cities moving. Electrification is a prime concern, like the Cross City Scheme from Lichfield to Redditch through the heart of Birmingham. This will be run in conjunction with Centro, the West Midlands PTE. New Class 323s will reduce noise and pollution and cut journey times by 15 minutes.

to the Midlands and North West, Liverpool to Norwich, Birmingham to Cardiff and Edinburgh to Glasgow are ideal for executive and leisure travel.

THE RURAL SERVICE

The Rural Service connects with InterCity and is often supported by a Local Authority. Lincolnshire gives enormous assistance to lines which would otherwise have to close. There may be a deficit but the service to the community and benefit to the environment greatly outweigh it. Regional Railways is improving urban and rural transport, benefiting our lifestyle and environment by helping to reduce energy-wasteful road vehicles.

"The Rural Service keeps villages and small towns linked to larger population areas"

THE INTERURBAN SERVICE

The Interurban Service provides long distance trains linking major cities and towns. There is huge scope for business travel and fast trains such as Newcastle to Liverpool, South Wales

Combined with PTE and light rail services locally and InterCity services naturally, Regional Railways is helping to fulfil the increasing need for fast rail travel across Britain. The potential is unlimited.

GIONAL RAILWAYS

The 90 m.p.h. Class 158 includes BT card telephones and full facilities for the disabled and for nursing mothers

Centro is committed to a high quality rail
network that drivers will choose to use

Taking people out of cars means
more road space for those who
have to use them

Strathclyde PTE have a light rail
system scheduled for the
Glasgow connurbations

The link between economic
progress and more cars has to
be broken in the interests of the
entire nation

PTEG
PASSENGER TRANSPORT EXECUTIVE GROUP

LOCAL RAIL INFORMATION

Travel shops give information on services

PTE's were formed under the Transport Act 1968 to plan and provide integrated public transport.

Yorkshire, Greater Manchester, Merseyside and West Midlands. PTE'S are financed by Transport Passenger

"Without PTE'S suburban rail services outside London might have withered away."

There are seven based on the provincial conurbations: Tyne & Wear, Strathclyde, West Yorkshire, South

Authorities made up of local councillors. They promote schemes to provide a fairer transport system for everyone

At the heart of Merseytravel's electrified network is a £34m centralised control and communications system

All of South Yorkshire's major population areas are within 30 minutes by rail of the £400m Meadowhall shopping complex

Strathclyde Regional council have invested £460m in the local rail network over the last 20 years

supporting rail and bus services essential to the community but not viable commercially. There is concessionary travel for the elderly, disabled and young people as well as services for the mobility handicapped.

Most PTE trains are operated by Regional Railways - with trains decked in special liveries.

PTE'S buy £250m worth of services from British Rail each year - that's 1.7 million trains carrying 156 million passengers with an income of £105m. Their capital expenditure on railways is £100m.

PTE's provide an input into District Council planning. They are a leading force in providing light rail along with other emergent schemes to free cities of motor traffic and provide a pleasanter, healthier environment in which energy is conserved and the motor car is not allowed to dominate everyday life.

TYNE & WEAR

Tyne & Wear achieved worldwide fame by creating an integrated transport system with Britain's first light rail network as its backbone. Built largely over former B.R. tracks work began in 1974 and today the system is 37 miles long with 46 stations.

An extension has recently been opened to Newcastle Airport and a new line to Sunderland is soon to be built.

STRATHCLYDE

Strathclyde Regional Council is Europe's largest Local Authority. Good public transport is essential and Strathclyde has the most extensive rail network outside London. There are 159 stations and ScotRail operate the service.

Strathclyde Regional Council are proud of the achievements they have made in providing the region with a superb railway network including 20 stations reopened.

> *"Strathclyde PTE aims to have 95 per cent of Glasgow's population within walking distance of a station"*

WEST YORKSHIRE

Metro is the product of good local government: the five districts, Bradford, Calderdale, Kirklees, Leeds and Wakefield, combining through the PTA to provide a dynamic transport system.

Exciting new projects include the Leeds and Bradford electrification and resignalling which will extend up the Aire and Wharf Valleys to Ilkley and Skipton.

Since the Glasgow Underground was modernised in 1980, patronage has doubled

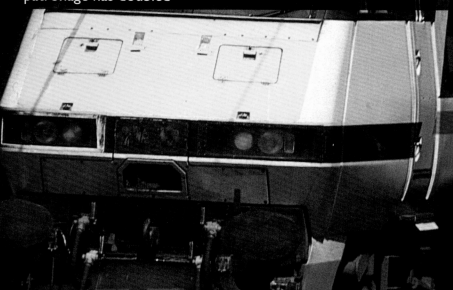

Greater Manchester's Metrolink routes are linked by tracks running on-street through the heart of the city

SOUTH YORKSHIRE

South Yorkshire PTE's aim is car competitive public transport and 150 per cent increase in rail patronage has been made over the last five years.

Building of Sheffield's Super Tram Light Rail Network has been a model for authorities to emulate nationwide.

GREATER MANCHESTER

The Metrolink Light Rail system is another triumph of local government. It was built on two existing commuter lines, Altrincham to Deansgate and Bury to Victoria.

By linking with Regional Railways and InterCity, Metrolink proves the unlimited potential for railway development.

MERSEYTRAVEL

Expansion of the electrified network is a top priority, with a £12 million scheme linking the major centres of Chester and Ellesmere Port to the Wirral Line.

Studies are also underway into the electrification of the trans-Pennine route from Liverpool to Newcastle.

28 older stations are earmarked for extensive refurbishment.

WEST MIDLANDS

The Current cost of road congestion in the West Midlands is £600m a year - a figure which could rise to £2bn in twenty years time - that is equivalent to scrapping a new Ford Sierra every three minutes.

> *"Metrolink heralds the return of trams to Manchester after 43 years"*

Europe's busiest diesel operated commuter line, the cross city Lichfield to Redditch has been electrified. Centro has also opened new stations.

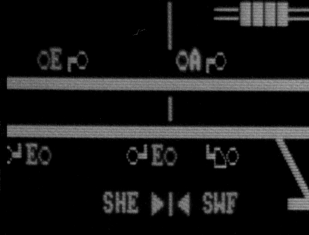

Central Services have developed the Stoneblower for track maintenance

The Test Car "Mentor" checks overhead catenary throughout the system

Fine dry snow swirling at high velocity around electrical systems is another area of research

Central Services

The six main Businesses of British Rail own their own trains, track, depots, personnel and other assets, Central Services provides strategic support with a diverse range of specialised skills.

The guardians of safety are well-maintained rolling stock advanced signalling and high-quality track; all can be produced or monitored by Central Services.

Comfort depends on coach design and track condition. Coach interiors are being developed; seating ergonomically-designed with room to spread out and yet be intimate enough to be able to talk or work with fellow-travellers. Floor and wall carpeting and innovative lighting are also essential.

> *"Central Services designed and developed electronic signalling systems lead the world"*

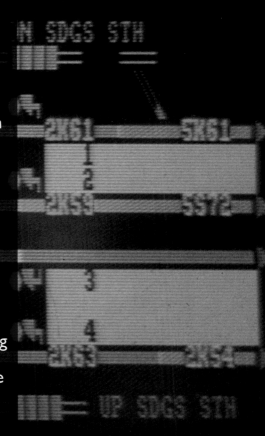

Contact with the rail is through the bogie which needs to be robust, flexible and well-sprung. Researchers are developing bogies which are 30% lighter with 40% less aerodynamic drag, saving energy, minimising track damage and the transmission of noise throughout the coach. External noise is also measured in the search to produce quieter trains.

No coach will provide comfort without good track. High speed recording vehicles monitor its condition and pass information to the Permanent Way Engineer of the Business concerned.

Safety and comfort mean little without reliability which is, best achieved by "Whole Train Intelligence" under which an on-board computer registers the mechanical and electrical conditions. Faults are anticipated, enabling maintenance to be on a "condition determined basis" rather than a random mileage one.

The menace of wheelslip caused by autumn leaves getting crushed on the rails is another area of research. It's a problem suffered by railways worldwide, especially those running multiple-units with light axle loadings.

Test cars measure vehicle performance comparing in reality to what was expected in design. The information

The Architecture and Design Group renovate old stations which need sensitive modernisation

is analysed by on-board computers and decoded at Derby Technical Centre. Similar tests are carried out to ensure that new vehicles are safe to run on the railway.

The Works Division produces long welded rail, points and crossings, creosoted timber sleepers, ballast from Meldon Quarry, steel and concrete bridges and fits track layouts to the correct clearances.

They also maintain signal and telecommunications equipment.

The "Stoneblower" injects new ballast beneath the sleepers and the track bed remains firm up to 3 times longer than with tamping.

Electronic signalling is being developed. Solid-state interlocking with microchips reduces costs and improves reliability compared with the large mechanical relay rooms in signal boxes.

Integrated Electronic Control Centres are designed and project-managed. At London's Liverpool Street VDU's show track diagrams and train whereabouts over 50 route miles.

The centre at Gateshead is state of the art; it contains over half of the world's solid-state interlocking equipment and controls 700 signals and 400 sets of points over 200 route kilometres using

Fire-resistant materials for coach seats are rigorously tested by Central Services

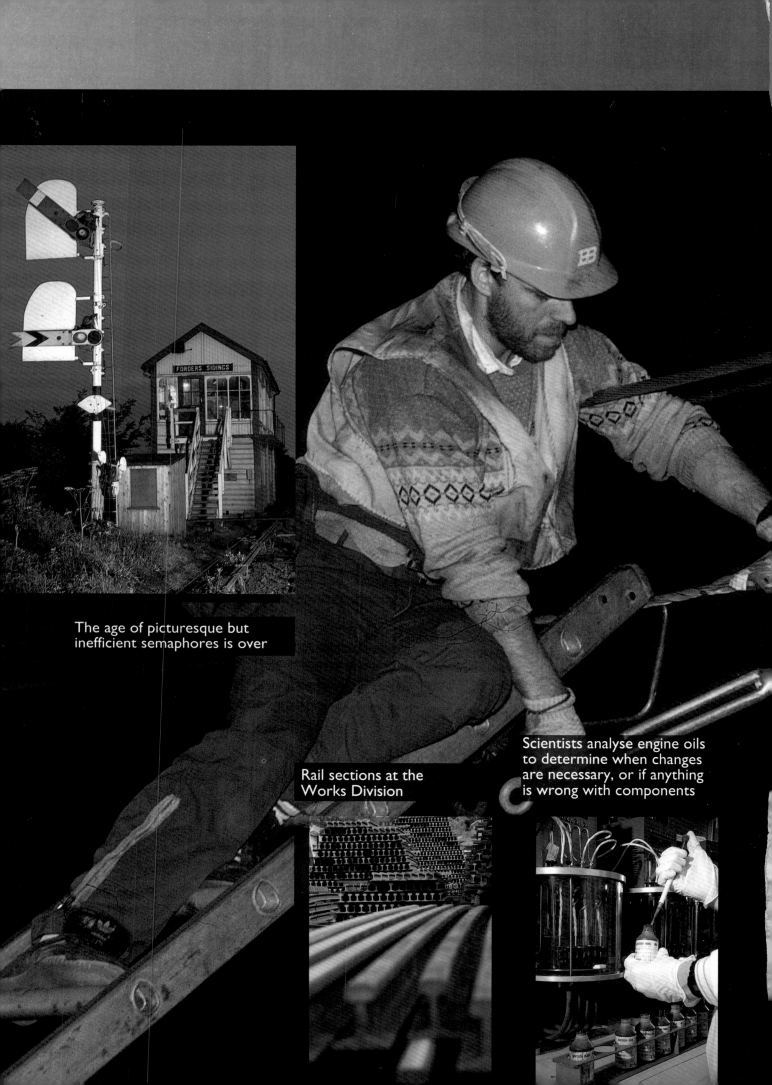

The age of picturesque but
inefficient semaphores is over

Rail sections at the
Works Division

Scientists analyse engine oils
to determine when changes
are necessary, or if anything
is wrong with components

Gateshead Electronic Control Centre controls 700 signals and 400 sets of points over 200 route kilometres

Automatic ticketing systems are developed by Central Services

only 3 signalmen. Train paths are set, delays minimised and information given to passengers.

Improved pathing makes the railway safer and able to take more trains. An important factor in traffic-ridden Britain and a key element in the formation of a coherent transport policy.

Other aspects of Central Services include: track safety advice, personnel computer systems, rolling stock procurement, vehicle spares supply, electrical power contracts, pensions management, infrastructure fleet management, civil engineering, supply trains, prototype vehicle build, project management, ticketing systems at stations, timetable production and mainframe computer systems.

"The future of Britain's Railway is researched, developed and supported by Central Services."

British Rail is one of the world's leading networks and Central Services, with its high technology skills, provides assistance worldwide on all hi-tech activities relating to the running of a modern efficient railway.

STREET CRANE Co. Ltd.
S.W.L. 7.5 TONNES
1988 No. 7014

2

INTERCITY

After overhaul, the bogies are refitted to the body before the vehicle is transferred to the paintshop

BRML

British Rail Maintenance Limited (BRML) was formed in 1987 to provide dedicated facilities for overhaul and repair of locomotives, coaches and multiple units from its four sites at Eastleigh, Wolverton, Springburn and Doncaster.

"All four of BRML's sites - along with its H.Q. in Derby - have achieved full certification in BS5750 accreditation"

In general terms Eastleigh is responsible for electric multiple units; Wolverton for coaching stock, Springburn and Doncaster for locomotives and diesel multiple units.

Eastleigh is the largest of BRML's sites and is almost exclusively involved in the maintenance and repair of Network SouthEast's large fleet of passenger vehicles.

A wide variety of diesel multiple units are overhauled

The pistons are lifted from the power unit of a diesel electric locomotive during overhaul

A first generation DMU - over 30 years old - is overhauled at Doncaster

and painted at Doncaster. There is an overnight bogie change facility for Sprinter Units with vehicles coming in after the evening rush and returned to service for the morning peak.

Much of Wolverton's business centres around the overhaul of Mark 3 coach sets which form the backbone of InterCity's Passenger Fleet.

buffet/kitchen which the Wolverton Depot overhauls every million miles, the task must be completed within twenty days so intensively are these high speed trains used.
The bodies are lifted from the bogies and placed on stands - the bodies and bogies being overhauled simultaneously.

The bogies are dismantled and cleaned;

"Two yearly overhauls on Sprinters are now turned around overnight between the evening and morning peak services"

Each of these high speed diesel trains usually comprises two power cars and eight coaches. It is the rakes of these coaches including first, standard and

wheels are checked and profile turned if necessary. All axles undergo ultrasonic tests to ensure there are no defects.

InterCity coach overhaul at Wolverton

Locomotives overhauled at Doncaster range from Class 31s built in the 1950s, to the latest Class 91 InterCity 225

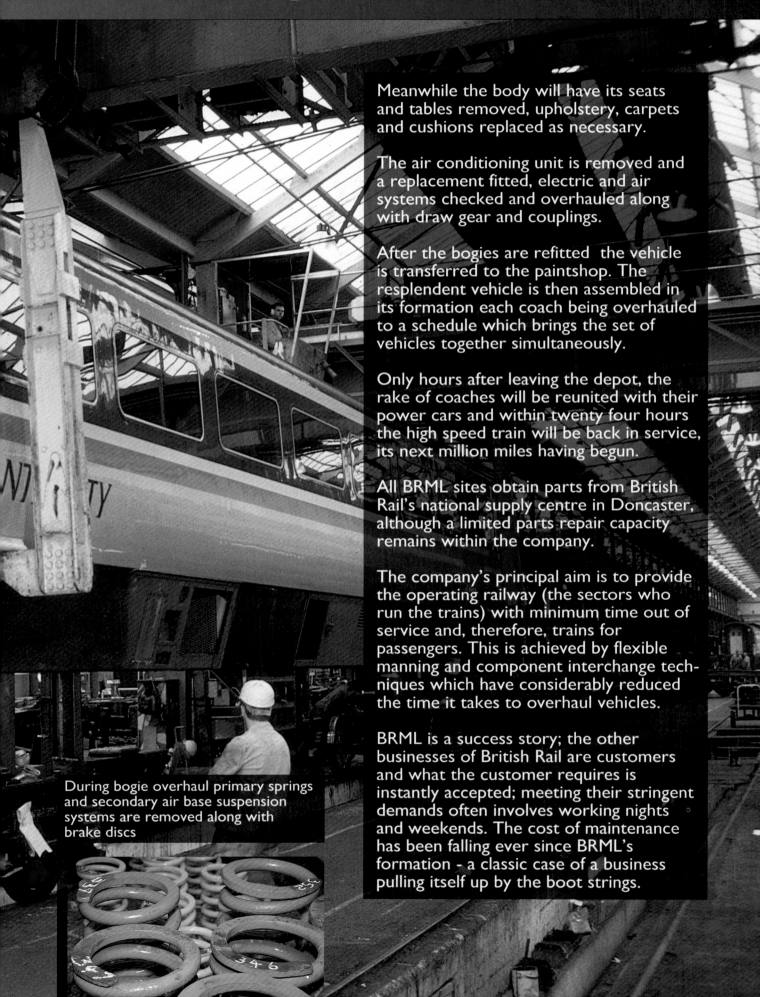

Meanwhile the body will have its seats and tables removed, upholstery, carpets and cushions replaced as necessary.

The air conditioning unit is removed and a replacement fitted, electric and air systems checked and overhauled along with draw gear and couplings.

After the bogies are refitted the vehicle is transferred to the paintshop. The resplendent vehicle is then assembled in its formation each coach being overhauled to a schedule which brings the set of vehicles together simultaneously.

Only hours after leaving the depot, the rake of coaches will be reunited with their power cars and within twenty four hours the high speed train will be back in service, its next million miles having begun.

All BRML sites obtain parts from British Rail's national supply centre in Doncaster, although a limited parts repair capacity remains within the company.

The company's principal aim is to provide the operating railway (the sectors who run the trains) with minimum time out of service and, therefore, trains for passengers. This is achieved by flexible manning and component interchange tech- niques which have considerably reduced the time it takes to overhaul vehicles.

BRML is a success story; the other businesses of British Rail are customers and what the customer requires is instantly accepted; meeting their stringent demands often involves working nights and weekends. The cost of maintenance has been falling ever since BRML's formation - a classic case of a business pulling itself up by the boot strings.

During bogie overhaul primary springs and secondary air base suspension systems are removed along with brake discs

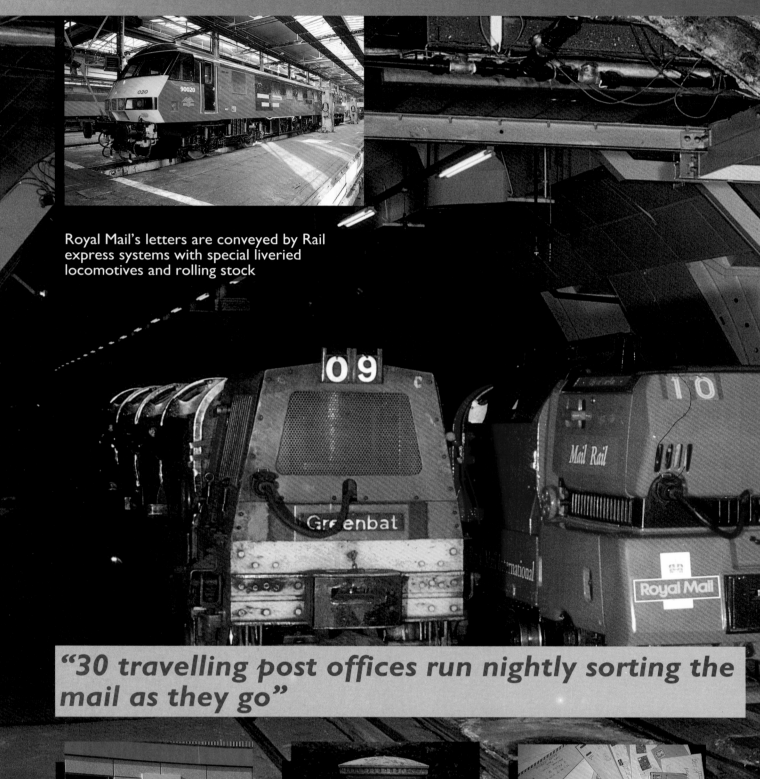

Royal Mail's letters are conveyed by Rail express systems with special liveried locomotives and rolling stock

"30 travelling post offices run nightly sorting the mail as they go"

Rail express systems

Red Star has 250 parcel points, open 24 hours, 7 days a week, nationwide.

Parcels Sector comprises two dynamic operations: Rail Express systems and Red Star. Over one hundred trains run nightly carrying over fifteen million letters - thirty are travelling post offices which sort the mail as they go.

Lines, along with routes to the South. Royal Mail's underground 'Mailraïl' which runs from Whitechapel to Paddington may be extended to Willesden reducing road delays and providing a properly coordinated rail system for London's mail.

"100 m.p.h. running gives rail the competitive edg

One hundred miles-per-hour running gives rail the competitive edge for long distance journeys, as mail must arrive by 3.00 a.m. in time for final sorting and delivery.

Over one-third of Britain's mail passes through London and a giant terminal is planned at Willesden next to the West Coast Main Line and the North Circular Road. This terminal will distribute nationwide via the East and West Coast and Great Western Main

Red Star maintains a large share of the parcels market, by providing a same day delivery with 125 m.p.h. trains - timings no one can match.

Packages can either be taken to your local office or collected. As an example items handed to Red Star in Leicester at 10.30 a.m. can be delivered (or collected) same day in: Birmingham-1250; London- 1330; Newcastle-1550; or Norwich- 1600. No road based haulier can offer a comparable service.

Freight of all sizes is carried in containers, swapbody units of conventional wagons

RfD is the market leader in the inland distribution of ocean-going containers

Many trains operate at night providing an unrivalled service unaffected by weather, traffic congestion and road repairs

Railfreight Distribution

Almost 300 timetabled trains run daily

Railfreight Distribution (RfD) carries 15m tonnes of cargo annually.

The Channel Tunnel will herald a potential new age for RfD. Overnight Britain's 15,000 kilometre network will be joined to a powerful 240,000 kilometres of pan-European railway offering fast, direct and congestion

daily, running at speeds up to 90 m.p.h.: Manchester to Milan in 32 hours, London to Munich in 24 hours, Cardiff to Paris in 15 hours.

This could be the equivalent of 400,000 lorry loads from road to rail reducing pollution, congestion, road building and accidents.

"No system could be simpler or more efficient than trains speeding from a rail connected terminal or factory direct to their destination"

free rail access to the prime markets of the European mainland.

RfD will have the capacity to operate 70 direct international freight trains

There will be nine regional intermodal centres for moving container and swapbody trains for Europe located in Scotland, the North East, North West, West Midlands and London.

One aggregate train can replace 185 lorries

Trainload Freight is Britain's biggest haulier and British Rail's most profitable business. Its trains carry 120 m tonnes a year, the equivalent of 5 million lorry loads, which parked nose to tail would encircle the globe!

Trainload Freight is responsible for 2,600 kilometres of track and uses 15,000 belonging to other rail businesses; it employs 13,000 people and has 400 mainline locomotives at 25 depots. There are 11 wagon repair centres, 50 train crew points and it serves over 700 private sidings and terminals.

"One aggregate train can replace 185 lorries"

Investment has been made in new depots and locomotives, including 100 Class 60s. These can haul 4,000 tonnes and during their projected life the fleet of 60s could haul 2,000 m tonnes – 25 times the weight of Ben Nevis.

062

TANK CAR
READY FO

COLLECTIO

Trainload Freight is organised around 4 industry–related profit centres: COAL, CONSTRUCTION, METAL, PETROLEUM. The largest is coal with some 200 locomotives. Most operate a merry–go–round, loading and discharging

"Trainload freight moves vast tonnages around the country virtually unnoticed and with minimal affect on the environment"

on the move from colliery to power station and back operations which generate half of Britain's electricity.

Trainload Freight's largest industry—related profit centre is coal with some 200 locomotives and a staff of almost 5,000

Above: One of the Trainload Coal's merry—go—round trains which load and discharge on the move from colliery to power station and back
Below: Most aggregates go to the southeast principal sources: ARC and Foster Yeoman in Somerset

Many power stations like Ratcliffe, West Burton and Rugeley burn up to 5 m tonnes a year, whilst Drax burns over 10 m tonnes and needs 30 trains a day. Coal trains also serve cement, steel, paper and chemical plants.

Trainload Constructions carries aggregates, domestic waste, soil and cement.

Trainload Metals carries 17 m tonnes a year; 70 per cent in raw materials – iron ore and limestone – and 30 per cent in semi–finished commodities. Imported iron ore is conveyed from Immingham Docks to Scunthorpe and from Port Talbot to Llanwern.

Rationalisations in the steel industry have left some rolling mills and coating plants remote from the steel works and Trainload Freight provides a moving conveyor between them.

Trainload Petroleum plays a vital role in the oil industry. It has to be competitive as the customer can use road, pipeline or coastal shipping. Main flows are from coastal refineries to distribution terminals. Crude oil from on shore fields is also conveyed to refineries. The hauls from Humberside to Langley in West London are a famous part of the railway scene with 2,000 tonne trains.

The movement of waste by rail provides an environmentally friendly answer to one of the sensitive problems of disposal

Hot steel at 450°C is loaded directly into 102 tonne wagons at the rolling mill

Trainload Petroleum serves all but one of the major oil companies

Almost half a million commuters are carried to London daily with peak hour trains arriving every 11 seconds. It is Europe's most intensive peak period operation

Network SouthEast is one of the largest retail operators in the southeast

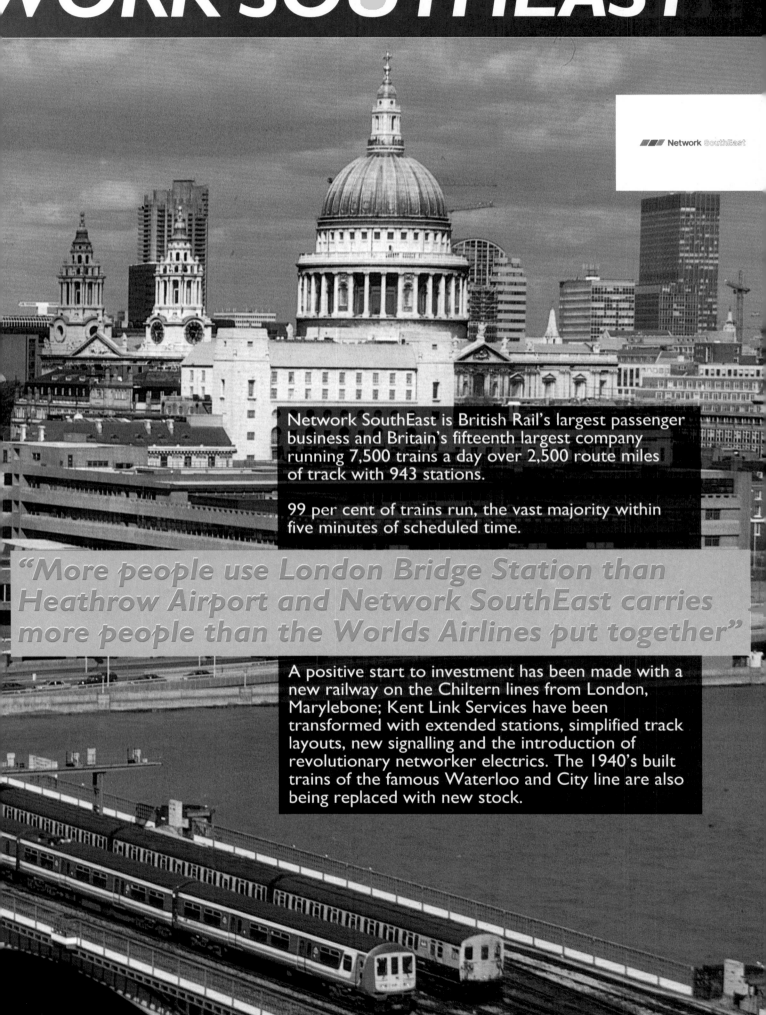

Network SouthEast

Network SouthEast is British Rail's largest passenger business and Britain's fifteenth largest company running 7,500 trains a day over 2,500 route miles of track with 943 stations.

99 per cent of trains run, the vast majority within five minutes of scheduled time.

"More people use London Bridge Station than Heathrow Airport and Network SouthEast carries more people than the Worlds Airlines put together"

A positive start to investment has been made with a new railway on the Chiltern lines from London, Marylebone; Kent Link Services have been transformed with extended stations, simplified track layouts, new signalling and the introduction of revolutionary networker electrics. The 1940's built trains of the famous Waterloo and City line are also being replaced with new stock.

Some Network SouthEast trains are almost 40 years old and a coordinated investment programme is essential

Facilities for the disabled exist throughout the Network

Travelcard combining bus, tube and train has attracted many people from road to rail, particularly leisure travellers who account for half of Network SouthEast's ticket revenue.

Network SouthEast has many exciting visions. The Heathrow Express would be a 100 m.p.h. super train which would whisk customers between Paddington and the airport in 16 minutes. Providing

"Unless the core network is maintained London's credibilty as a business and financial centre will be threatened"

finance is raised, trains could be running in 1997.

Whether building new stations or restoring our Victorian heritage, Network's architects have created a cheerful welcoming style

CrossRail is a £1.8bn scheme to provide twin tunnels under London linking Network SouthEast services at Paddington with Liverpool Street.

provide a new low level station beneath the existing one that would link with international trains to Europe. King's Cross would be the

> "Network SouthEast operates as 9 separate divisions each with its own management"

With a journey time of only ten minutes, travellers will be able to cross London from the east and west suburbs direct to the City and West End – Bond Street, Oxford Circus and Faringdon.

hub of Britain's railway network by providing easy access from InterCity's West Coast, Midland and East Coast Mainlines, Thameslink 2000's routes and European Services running via Britain's proposed high speed link to

> "London's road congestion crisis is costing the British economy £10bn per year– CBI figures."

Thameslink the successful North to South route through London has potential to expand its services by 40 per cent. Under a vision known as Thameslink 2000, up to 24 trains an hour could run from destinations as diverse as King's Lynn, Portsmouth, Huntingdon and Faversham – all through the heart of London.

Thameslink 2000 is intended to form part of the King's Cross project to

the tunnel. An interchange at Faringdon with CrossRail would open up the whole of London North to South and East to West.

The capital's main airports, Heathrow, Gatwick, Luton and Stansted would also be efficiently connected.

WORK SOUTHEAST

800 new coaches have been put into service since the Network was formed in 1986

Given the will and investment, London's railways could solve the congestion crisis and become Europe's most advanced commuter system

The new international terminal at London Waterloo from which the Eurostar services to Europe will operate

SSENGER SERVICES

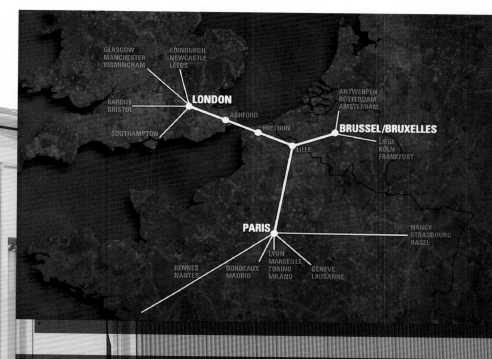

A SERVICE THAT OPENS UP EUROPE
A breakthrough in direct travel between London and Paris or Brussels is poised to happen in 1994. The

"The Channel Tunnel heralds the greatest opportunity for our railway this century."

breakthrough is Eurostar. A direct journey through the Channel Tunnel from London Waterloo International to Paris Gare du Nord will take just three hours and from London Waterloo International to Brussels, Bruxelles Midi three and a quarter hours. International terminals will be easy to use, new and spacious.

The Eurostar train sets new standards in technological sophistication. The trains will be capable of travelling at 185 m.p.h. With Eurostar ideas of time and distance change, barriers disappear.

This unique event in European service has required

The International trains will be maintained at North Pole depot in West London

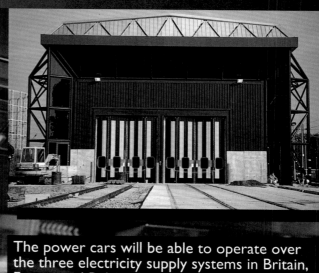

The power cars will be able to operate over the three electricity supply systems in Britain, France and Belgium

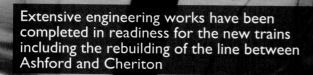

Extensive engineering works have been completed in readiness for the new trains including the rebuilding of the line between Ashford and Cheriton

considerable investment in track, terminals, depots, bridges, signalling and electrification

International travel to mainland Europe will be convenient and easy. In 1995 it will be possible to travel on Eurostar between Paris or Brussels and the Midlands, the North or Scotland. International night services will also serve those places and run to and from Wales and the West Country. Other night services will link London and the Netherlands or Germany. Choose a destination and going there will be easy.

Travel will be fast, direct and relaxing. In first class a meal may be served at your seat. In other carriages there will be nappy changing facilities, family areas and a welcoming bar buffet.

Eurostar is the creation of European Passenger Services, a wholly owned subsidiary of British Rail, along with the national railways of France (SNCF) and Belgium (SNCB\SNCM).

The breakthrough begins in 1994.

During the 1960s Beeching closed 50 per cent of Britain's railway network. His actions still evoke feelings of anger and revulsion nationwide

BRITAIN'S RAILWAY

101 361

Britain's railway is an illustration of how a bureaucratic monolith can be transformed into one of Britain's leading businesses. This achievement resulted mainly from the 1992 reorganisation "Organisation for Quality".

"The spectre of another Beeching holocaust stalks the land"

At one time or another, most of us have attacked our nationalised industries for being inefficient, overstaffed and a waste of public money. Certainly the privatisation of many of these industries has proved successful in transforming them into viable businesses. British Rail, however, does not fall into this category.

"We must not allow our railway to be fragmented by cherry picking cowboys and property sharks who have no inherent interest in the industry"

Privatisation would lead to a contraction of the service, as

unprofitable lines would be shut down at a social and environmental cost to our national infrastructure. Investment in new rolling stock, track and signalling would be postponed — at enormous risk to safety and

"Government plans to halve BR's borrowing powers will decimate our railway's capacity to provide a civilised alternative to burgeoning road traffic"

service — in an effort to appease the City with healthy profits and dividends. British Rail's achievement should be commended and they should be encouraged to improve their service even more. Investment should be a priority. Then, once again, we can demonstrate that British ingenuity and expertise, channelled correctly, is the best in the world and gain valuable exports from the manufacture of new equipment.

Will the only trains in the 21st Century be those operated by enthusiasts?

BRITAIN'S RAILWAY

This book is based on the 12-Projector Multi-Vision Audio-Visual Theatre Production *Britain's Railway* which is regularly playing in theatres, schools, leisure centres and clubs across the nation.

It is a unique production running for over two hours, revealing in detail, sector by sector, the achievements and aspirations of British Rail. The show contains 4,000 beautifully composed images, computer programmed to a superb stereo sound-track. During the performance 54 carousel tray changes are made.

The show was produced by Milepost 92½ and during the two-year production period, Milepost's photographers travelled 300,000 miles over all sectors of the British Rail Network and shot 2,000 rolls of Agfachrome film.

The production's original purpose was to present the case for railways and help redress the often biased and unfair coverage given to our railway by many sections of the media - particularly the tabloids. Since the launch in October 1992, the situation facing our railway has become increasingly ominous and the show plays to packed audiences interested to assess the true value to the nation of a properly coordinated railway run by professionals, many of whom are devoted to the industry they serve.

It would be impossible to tour a show of this complexity without considerable backing and Milepost wishes to thank Agfa, Canon and Electrosonic.

MILEPOST

Milepost 92½ is comprised of a team of talented individuals, led by Colin Garratt, specialising in Audio-Visual production, Photographic Services and Picture Library for the railway, transport and leisure industries.

For full information on Milepost 92½ along with bookings and enquiries for *Britain's Railway*, please contact:

Milepost 92½
Newton Harcourt
Leicestershire
LE8 0FH

Tel: 0533 592068
Fax: 0533 593001